Original title:
Floral Fantasy

Copyright © 2025 Creative Arts Management OÜ
All rights reserved.

Author: Derek Caldwell
ISBN HARDBACK: 978-1-80566-787-2
ISBN PAPERBACK: 978-1-80566-807-7

The Language of Wildflowers

In a field of whispers, petals argue,
One says, 'I'm the prettiest, that's true!'
While daisies giggle, making quite a fuss,
'Come on, you know we're all fabulous!'

Buttercups prance with a sunny delight,
In shades of yellow, they're ready to fight.
But lilacs swoon, smelling so divine,
'Chill out, my friends, let's sip some sunshine!'

Petals that Paint the Dawn

Morning yawns with a splash of hues,
As flowers shake off their nightly snooze.
'Are you ready to dazzle?' the tulips plead,
'Let's show the world we're quite the breed!'

The sun stretches, tickling every leaf,
While roses giggle, 'What a silly chief!'
'Hope he remembers our morning tea,
With honey from bees and laughter for free!'

A Cascade of Color

In a garden jungle, colors collide,
With violets taunting the sunlight outside.
'Look at us all, we're nature's jesters!'
Blossoms reply, 'We're the true investors!'

Zinnias dance like they own the place,
Their wild moves can put others to disgrace.
Petunias chuckle, 'Oh, what a show!'
While sunflowers roll, 'Let's steal the glow!'

Butterfly Kisses on Dewdrops

Butterflies flutter, wearing spots and stripes,
Chasing dew on petals, making silly gripes.
'You're too slow!' one teases with flair,
While daisies giggle, 'Try flying in air!'

'The early bird gets the worm, they say,'
But butterflies know it's just child's play.
With kisses on petals, the jokes abound,
While nature chuckles at the silliness found!

Chasing the Horizon of Blooms

In a field where daisies dance,
Bumblebees took a silly chance.
They wobbled high, they trembled low,
Chasing a breeze, oh what a show!

With sunhats made of clover green,
They twirled in circles, quite the scene!
A butterfly busts out a giggle,
As they bump and bounce, oh how they wiggle!

Giggles echo through the air,
As sunflowers start to do the fair.
They think they're tall, and oh, so bright,
But wind blows them sideways, what a sight!

The horizon spills with colors bright,
As flowers fret in morning light.
They chase their shadows, what a chase!
In fields of fun, they find their place!

Lavenders Sing Under the Moon

Underneath the silver glow,
Lavenders hum a tune so slow.
With petals soft, they tease the night,
Swaying gently, what a sight!

A chorus of bees joins in the fun,
Rubbing their legs, they've just begun.
With tiny hats, they gather around,
To buzz in rhythm, oh such sound!

Crickets stop to lend an ear,
They laugh and chirp, full of cheer.
Lavenders twirl in fragrant glee,
With melodies danced on the breeze!

Oh, the moon winks with delight,
As flowers giggle, oh so bright.
In a garden where jokes take flight,
Lavenders sing until first light!

The Garden's Hidden Palette

In corners where the daisies jest,
The garden keeps its secrets best.
With every shade, a laugh appears,
Painted petals hide their cheers.

Pansies pout with playful grins,
While violets tease with purple spins.
The tulips giggle, standing tall,
They trip and stumble, bound to fall!

Sunflowers peek from behind the gate,
Making faces, it's never late.
A riot of colors, what a crew,
Each blossom with a joke or two!

As the sun dips low in the west,
The garden's palette brings the jest.
In petals bright, the humor's sown,
Where laughter blooms, it feels like home!

Roses Wrapped in Moonlight

Roses wrapped in moonlit threads,
Chat and giggle from their beds.
With every rustle, a joke takes flight,
Tickling the stars, what a sight!

Thorns stand guard, but join the fun,
Rolling their eyes as roses run.
They sway and sway, oh what a dare,
Budding jokes drift through the air!

The moon beams down, a silver grin,
As petals whisper, "Let's begin!"
Each punchline lands, a bloom of glee,
In the garden, wild and free!

The night unfolds with giggles bright,
As roses dance in the pale light.
With laughter wrapped in fragrant rhyme,
They celebrate this joyful time!

Whispers of Petals

A daisy sneezes, oh what a sight,
The tulips giggle, oh what delight!
Sunflowers gossip, heads held high,
Cheerful blooms laughing, oh my, oh my!

Bumblebees buzz, with secrets they share,
Carnations in pink just can't help but stare.
Roses like jesters, wearing bright grins,
Petals in chaos, let the fun begin!

Marigolds prance, with skirts made of cheer,
Jokes in the garden, come gather, my dear.
Dandelions dance, the wind is their friend,
Whispers of petals, let humor transcend!

Dreaming in Bloom

In a meadow where laughter roams free,
Tulips tell tales, with glee, oh so glee!
Sunshine hats on, they laugh and they play,
Petals in pajamas, what a bright day!

A daffodil trips, falls over its shoe,
Laughter erupts, as the daisies say, 'Boo!'
With every breeze, the garden erupts,
In this lively show, who's the next to disrupt?

Butterflies giggle, all dressed up in flair,
Joking with bees, here and there in the air.
A jug of sunlight, they sip kind of slow,
In a dream full of giggles, where funny seeds grow!

The Garden's Secret Symphony

In the garden at dusk, a concert begins,
Petals like drummers, oh how they spin!
The roses compose a sweet serenade,
While daisies perform in a dazzling parade.

A trumpet of pansies, a chorus of blooms,
Sunflowers spinning, busting out tunes.
Laughter erupts with each note they play,
In this symphony bright, let's dance all day!

Crickets join in with a soft, funny hum,
A raucous ensemble, oh here they come!
Garden songs will tickle your feet,
When flowers and laughter create such a beat!

Dances Beneath the Blossoms

Underneath branches where blossoms sway,
The flowers all gather, to party and play.
With petals that swirl and twirl like a dream,
They waltz in the moonlight, a whimsical theme.

Lilies in line dance, shoes made of dew,
While orchids bring snacks, there's much fun to chew!
The violets giggle, tripping over their toes,
In this jolly dance beneath the moon's glow.

Every bee claps with a buzzing sound,
As blossoms unite, in joy unbound.
Laughter and petals, all shining so bright,
In the garden of fun, everything feels right!

Enchanted Meadows

In meadows bright, the daisies dance,
They've planned a ball, and all in a trance.
The tulips twirl with hats on their heads,
While purple pansies snore in their beds.

A butterfly juggles, and bees play chess,
The sun turns up in a polka-dot dress.
A rabbit hops in, he's late yet again,
He trips on a thistle, oh, what a pain!

The grass whispers secrets, giggles ignite,
A ladybug jokes, oh what a delight!
The lilies chuckle, their petals aglow,
As the wind tells a story, just listen and know!

In this realm of cheer, all worries abide,
Where blooms throw a party, and joy is the guide.
So join in the fun, let your heart be free,
In meadows of laughter, come dance with me!

The Hart of Every Dandelion

A dandelion puff declared with glee,
"I'm the tiniest heart, so wild and free!"
With seeds that scatter like thoughts in the air,
They tickle your nose, now that's quite a scare!

The bees in their buzz, they can't stop to chat,
They've got a full schedule, it's all about that.
The ants march along, in a briefcase they hold,
"Time is money!" they say, in a hushed, earnest fold.

The snail on a stroll, moves slower than light,
He's gathering tales in the shimmer of night.
While clovers conspire, wearing grins ever wide,
Planning a prank on the cat that resides.

Oh, dandelion dreams, all puffed up with flair,
You bounce in the breeze like you just don't care!
In the garden of giggles, with laughter aligned,
You're the heart of the fun that we always find.

Echoes of the Springtime Muse

The springtime muse whispers, with petals all bright,
"Let's paint the world silly, it'll be such a sight!"
With roses in hats, and the tulips in shoes,
Each bloom a comedian, sharing their views!

The violets gossip, a gossip-filled spree,
"Oh, did you hear the news? The poppies flew free!"
A sunflower waves, a sunbeam on high,
"I'm the tallest of all, can you see? My oh my!"

The breeze carries laughter, the clouds crack a smile,
As petals trip lightly, they dance for a while.
The crocus jumps in with a tumble and swirl,
Chasing after butterflies, giving a twirl.

In this playful haven where stories collide,
Where flowers are jesters, with laughter as guide.
So come join the romp, let your cares slip away,
In the echoes of spring, let our hearts laugh and play!

A Tangle of Color and Light

In a garden of socks and odd shoes,
Daisies wear hats, doing the blues.
Petunias gossip, spilling their tea,
While dandelions dance, wild and free.

A sunflower twirls in a sunbeam so bright,
While bees join the tango, buzzing with delight.
The gardener trips on a vine, oh dear!
Laughter erupts, let's dance without fear.

Tulips are giggling, peeking in rows,
As the clumsy wind tickles their toes.
Butterflies waltz on a spinny leaf,
Beware the snapdragon, it's downright brief!

In this patch of chaos, joy takes its flight,
Where petals and pollen create pure delight.
Every bloom is a joke, a laugh in the air,
Come join this party, if you dare!

Echoes of Pollen and Promise

Bumblebees hum a silly tune,
Hovering high like a playful balloon.
Lily pads slip with a giggling grin,
"Watch your step!" they tease, "don't fall in!"

Marigolds wink with their petals so bright,
Throwing a festoon of colors in flight.
"Oh dear!" said the rose, "do I smell bad?"
"Not at all!" said the lilac, "you're just a tad!"

A daffodil sneezes, oh how it goes,
Wiping its nose with a leaf, goodness knows!
Pansies in pairs burst into glee,
"Let's hold a party, just you and me!"

In the garden of laughter, all worries cease,
Where petals hug petals, and giggles increase.
A merry parade of colors at play,
Join in the fun, it's a bloom-filled day!

The Veil of a Flowered Dawn

Morning breaks with a riot of cheer,
Where tulips wear scarves, oh my, so queer!
A daisy in slippers hops with a grin,
While a poppy does ballet, twirling in spin.

A fragrant breeze whispers silly old rhymes,
As violets chuckle at the silliest times.
The sun peeks over, pulling out its rays,
Making dandelions dance in a daze.

Cacti are jealous; they can't bloom so wide,
While orchids giggle, bursting with pride.
A butterfly falls, with a fluttering flip,
"Don't mind me, friends, just grazing the tip!"

In this dawn of giggles and petals aglow,
Even the weeds join in, putting on a show.
The veil of laughter wraps around tight,
In this garden of dreams, everything's bright!

Cascading Hues of Playful Spirits

Roses in shades of raspberry swirl,
Giggle as daisies begin to twirl.
A jolly bluebell brings up the rear,
With a snicker and wink, it whispers, "Come near!"

Petals cascade like a colorful stream,
As squirrels debate if they can sing a dream.
"Oh, watch out!" yells a tulip on the run,
As a bumblebee tries to join in the fun.

Sunflowers gathered, their heads held so high,
Sharing tall tales as the clouds drift by.
The lively scent of nectar fills the air,
With hops and skips, there's laughter to share.

At the end of the day, the color parade,
Leaves echoes of joy that will never fade.
In a world stitched with giggles and light,
Cascading hues dance into the night!

Nightingale's Serenade in Lilac

In the garden, a nightingale sings,
Lilac whispers, oh, what joy it brings!
A little bee buzzes with delight,
Dancing 'round petals, oh what a sight!

The sunflowers chuckle, standing tall,
While tulips gossip, sharing it all.
A dandy lion rolls on the ground,
Saying, "Life's too short to wear a frown!"

Petals toss confetti in the air,
A rogue little gnome without a care.
He slips on a leaf, does a little jig,
Sprouting new moves, all sprightly and big!

As night falls, the moon takes a peek,
A giggling breeze makes flowers speak.
Laughter erupts from the lily pads,
Nature's concert, the best of fads!

The Enchanted Rosebud

A rosebud winks, oh what a tease,
With petals that dance in a playful breeze.
Thorns frown, but they can't spoil the fun,
As daisies and lilies join in the run!

Bouncing bumblebees wear tiny hats,
While butterflies spin in acrobat chats.
The snapdragons snap with a mighty roar,
As the garden erupts, laughing galore!

With each raindrop, squeaks of delight,
Twirling around, oh, what a sight!
The grasshoppers leap, in sync they prance,
Welcoming spring with a lively dance!

A mischievous squirrel steals a bloom,
Shakes it around in the twilight gloom.
With petals like ribbons, the flowers all cheer,
In this whimsical world, there's nothing to fear!

Petal Soft Murmurs

Petals whisper secrets to the sky,
Giggles of daisies, oh, so spry!
Tulips throw parties, with snacks galore,
"Come one, come all!" they cry and implore.

The wind, a jester, twirls around,
Tickling the petals that laugh, unbound.
"Who's got the best scent?" the flowers all debate,
As humidity rises, it's getting quite great!

A dainty fern rolls, catching the sun,
Taking a nap, oh, isn't it fun?
While clouds look down, they giggle and grin,
Sharing their fluff, like a cotton candy spin!

With lanterns of fireflies lighting the night,
All the blooms gather, it's quite a sight.
They trade their best jokes, each one a delight,
In this garden of laughter, everything feels right!

Moonlit Orchid Dreams

In the moonlight, orchids sway and sway,
Contemplating life in a dreamy way.
"Do we look better in shades of cream?
Or do we like violet more, or so it seems?"

A dandy lion whispers, "Who cares?"
"Let's skip the fuss, and let down our hairs!"
The nightingale chuckles with a melodic tune,
As fireflies twinkle, lighting the moon.

"Did you hear about the peony's riddle?"
"Oh please, do tell, I'm done with the fiddle!"
Their petals bloom wide, with laughter and glee,
As the whole garden joins in, can't you see?

The stars cast down giggles, so bright,
While the flowers dream of their next delight.
"It's a night of laughter, let's all sway!"
In moonlit mischief, let's dance away!

The Caress of a Petal's Touch

A dance of colors, bright and bold,
Petals giggle, stories told.
Bees in tuxedos, buzzing cheer,
Wearing pollen like it's their gear.

Sunlight tickles, laughter flows,
Daisies wink, as morning glows.
Butterflies play hide and seek,
On flowers' faces, joy they leak.

Stems whisper secrets, leafy cheer,
Tulips chuckle, 'Spring is here!'
Nature's jesters, round and spry,
In this garden, who'd deny?

A daffodil did a little dance,
Swaying left, giving chance.
To all the blooms in playful glee,
'Join the party!' shouts the bee.

Secrets Held Within Green Shadows

In shady nooks where blossoms peek,
Ladybugs laugh with utmost cheek.
Tall ferns whisper silly tales,
While vines giggle, weaving trails.

A rogue worm, with wiggles true,
Claims to be a plant in blue.
Cacti chortle, needles prick,
'This green game is quite the trick!'

Underneath the leafy dome,
Roaming beetles call it home.
In this kingdom, joy's the aim,
Every petal plays the game.

So gather 'round in green retreat,
Where flora and laughter meet.
Hidden jokes that nature shares,
In the shade, no one declares!

The Lexicon of Blossoms

Petunia jokes in purple prose,
While zinnias crack floral woes.
Chrysanthemums make rhymes with glee,
In a botanical jamboree!

Roses roll their eyes in jest,
'Get a grip, we're the best!'
Daffodils chime in, 'Oh please,
We're the fun-loving flowers, if you please!'

Hummingbirds chirp a catchy tune,
While pansies play a part-time rune.
Every leaf has something to say,
In this garden of dreams, come join the fray!

So pluck the humor, let it grow,
In every petal, laughter's glow.
For in this vibrant living space,
Nature's humor finds its place!

Beyond the Thorns of Desire

Thorns might poke, but what a game,
Blooming blooms, they feel the same.
A rose sneezes, petals fly,
Sending pollen on a high!

Budding friendships, all in bloom,
Witty lilacs share the room.
Petal pranks, a fragrant spree,
Smiling daisies dance with glee.

Whispered dreams through fragrant air,
Make weeding feel less like a care.
In this patch of joy we thrive,
Beyond the thorns, it's fun to strive!

So gather laughter, shed that fear,
In every flower, a giggle near.
Life's too short for drowsy plight,
Bloom with joy, let spirits light!

Wisteria's Gentle Embrace

Wisteria drapes from the sky,
Like a purple wig on a shy guy.
Bees are buzzing, trying to snack,
On sweet nectar, they've got no lack.

The vines twist and tangle with flair,
A floral game of hide and seek, beware!
A squirrel swings, with grace and leaps,
Chasing dreams through lavender heaps.

Beneath the blooms, a rabbit grins,
Fashioned in petals, a life to begin.
Dressed to impress, in shades so bright,
He hops on stage, a silly sight!

Oh, wisteria, with your playful jest,
Making every garden a grand fest.
With laughter swirling in every breeze,
You're the life of the floral tease!

Dreamscapes Beneath the Petals

Under bright blooms, the dreamers lie,
Pillows of petals sprinkle the sky.
Ladybugs dance on a soft, pink bed,
Wishing on beams from the sun's golden head.

A caterpillar scribbles a tale,
About pizza-flavored leaves on a trail.
While butterflies giggle and flutter near,
Wearing coats of colors, oh so dear!

In mossy spots, the fairies play,
Casting spells in a silly way.
With tiny giggles and playful twirls,
They turn the dirt into magical whirls.

Dreamscapes bloom where laughter reigns,
With flowers adorned in funny chains.
In a garden of whimsy, joy takes flight,
Under the stars, everything feels right!

The Secret Lives of Blossoms

Hush now, listen, the blossoms speak,
In whispers soft, their secrets peek.
They gossip about the bees at night,
Who steal their nectar, oh what a sight!

The roses argue; who's the fairest?
While daisies giggle, feeling the rarest.
Pansies prank the tulips with glee,
Dressing them up like a clown, you see!

Sunflowers boast of their height and might,
While violets are shy, avoiding the light.
Petunias laugh at the stiff old trees,
Swinging their heads in the soft summer breeze.

Such secret lives, a riotous show,
In the garden where laughter will grow.
With petals and leaves, they frolic and tease,
In nature's bright theater, they're sure to please!

Starlit Blossoms Unfold

When night falls, the blossoms awake,
With twinkling glimmers, they shimmy and shake.
Moonbeams tickle their soft, soft skin,
As they dance like mad, let the fun begin!

The daffodils don their sparkly caps,
Swing to the rhythm, no time for naps.
While tulips host a midnight show,
Sprinkling petals with a sprinkle of glow.

In the corner, a wild rose sings,
About mischief and magical things.
And with the stars as their guide and cheer,
They frolic and giggle, spreading the cheer!

Each starlit flower has a story to tell,
In a garden where giggles and joy swell.
With petals unfolding in moonlit grace,
The blooms come alive in this whimsical place!

The Dance of Wild Lilies

In the meadow, lilies twirl,
With petals that spin and swirl.
They giggle with the breeze so mild,
Dancing like a carefree child.

A bumblebee joins in the fun,
Zigzagging 'round like it's on the run.
The flowers chuckle, swaying bright,
In a playful, whimsical delight.

They plan a party for the sun,
Inviting clouds, oh what fun!
With sun hats made of dandelion,
Their revelry is quite defying.

At twilight, they do take a bow,
With rhymes that make the fireflies wow.
A raucous night, with stars up high,
Their sweet, silly joy fills the sky.

Symphony of Sunlit Gardens

In gardens warm, the flowers play,
With colors bold on bright display.
A sunflower makes a trumpet sound,
While daisies dance around the ground.

The roses wear their best attire,
To impress bees that never tire.
With a buzz and laugh, they all unite,
Creating music, pure delight.

A zinnia shouts, 'Let's have a race!'
While lilacs giggle at the pace.
The tulips cheer from their fine seats,
As blooms engage in silly feats.

At sunset's glow, they strike a pose,
With petals all in cheerful rows.
A symphony of joy is born,
In the garden where fun is sworn.

Moonlit Orchids

Under the moon, orchids beam,
Casting a light, a silvery dream.
They whisper jokes in the cooler air,
With giggles that float everywhere.

A moth joins in, dons a sleek tie,
As they dance in the night sky high.
Orchids wink, and the starlight's bright,
Turning the garden into a sight.

With petals soft and whispers sweet,
They jest about their evening feats.
The shadows chuckle, the night grows bold,
As their stories of madness unfold.

As dawn approaches, they snicker low,
"What fun we had, don't you know?"
With a final twirl and a happy sway,
The moonlit orchids bid goodbye to play.

A Tapestry of Color

In the garden, rainbow hues,
Each flower wears its lively shoes.
They share laughs and jests in the breeze,
Tickling the air with such sweet tease.

A marigold plays a prank with style,
While violets giggle all the while.
Petunias roll as if in glee,
Creating chaos—oh, how funny to see!

The geraniums blush with joy, oh dear,
At a joke that tickles every ear.
Chasing butterflies that buzz about,
With laughter echoing, there's no doubt.

As sunset comes, they laugh and sway,
In a colorful bloom ballet.
Their tapestry woven with vibrant bliss,
In a garden that delights with every kiss.

Whimsical Wonders of Verdant Realms

In gardens where the daisies dance,
A purple snail joins in the prance.
He wears a hat made out of leaves,
And giggles softly at the bees.

The tulips tease the passing ants,
With colorful jumps and silly chants.
They make up jokes about the sun,
As laughter spreads just like a bun.

A flower pot took up a drum,
And roared with laughter, oh so fun!
The violets rolled in fits of glee,
While wishing on a bumblebee.

But do beware the clumsy rose,
Who trips on petals, goodness knows!
With every tumble, blooms explode,
And paint the path in bright abode.

The Night Blooms In Harmony

At dusk, the moonbeams shed a light,
On petals dressed in silver bright.
The daisies hum a lullaby,
As nightingale soon flutters by.

In shadows, daisies share a joke,
A sunflower wears a threadbare cloak.
They giggle loud, oh what a sight,
As fireflies flash, igniting night.

A sleepy rose, with fuddled head,
Mistakes the wind for softest bed.
He snores so loud, the ivy shakes,
While all the blooms enjoy the breaks.

In tangled dreams, the petals twirl,
A waltz of colors, every swirl.
And laughter echoes through the trees,
In harmony with gentle breeze.

Petals Adrift on a Breeze

A dandelion floats by with grace,
Sipping on tea from a cozy place.
With every puff, it chuckles loud,
A wish on air, it feels so proud.

The roses trade their sweetest tales,
While butterflies don tiny sails.
They drift along, sharing a ride,
With giggles blooming far and wide.

A tulip tripped and did a spin,
While laughing at the world she's in.
She stumbled right into a pot,
And claimed it was a cozy spot!

The violets plan a grand parade,
With blossoms bright and routes well laid.
But oh dear me, the lilies sigh,
As all the blooms get stuck on high!

A Cascade of Wild Dreams

In fields of giggles, blossoms leap,
As fuchsia fairies start to creep.
They paint the air with laughter's brush,
And fill the meadow with a hush.

A wobbly daffodil on a bike,
Sails through the grass, a joyful hike.
With every pedal, laughter flies,
As passing bugs all gasp and sighs.

The lilacs dream of candy skies,
And lollipops that swell in size.
They giggle as they spin around,
Creating joy without a sound.

At last, the sun gives them a wink,
And leaves them twirling by the brink.
With every bloom, absurd it seems,
Life's wild fun is made of dreams.

A Compendium of Color

In gardens bright, the daisies dance,
Wearing hats in bold designs.
The tulips giggle, take a chance,
While roses sip on drink so fine.

Sunflowers wink from towers high,
With cheeky smiles across the way.
The violets plot, oh my, oh my,
For pranks to pull on bright bouquet.

Lilies laugh with fragrant flair,
Carts of pollen rolling through.
Dandelions float without a care,
As wild winds play tag, who knew?

Each hue a joke that nature plays,
In petals soft, a jest divine.
With buzzing bees, they mix their ways,
In laughter's hue, they intertwine.

A Revelation Wrapped in Green

The leaves are chatting, gossip spread,
In whispers soft of woodland dreams.
Old vines weave tales of joy instead,
While ferns spill secrets through their seams.

A crooked tree, a grinning stump,
Their roots entwined like old best friends.
With every thump and every jump,
The sun peeks in, the fun ascends.

In meadows, grasshoppers engage,
In hopping games to rule the day.
A squirrel strikes a pose on stage,
As nature's jesters laugh and play.

A hedgehog twirls, a berry feast,
Awkward moves bring peals of glee.
In every nook, there's laughter least,
A merry world, wild, bright, and free.

Petals in Twilight

When dusk sinks low, the petals speak,
In muted tones of purple haze.
The night unfolds, the blooms go meek,
Yet playtime lasts through twilight's maze.

A moonlit rose, a hazy blush,
With giggles floating in the air.
The poppies sway, a gentle hush,
While critters share a secret dare.

Daisies don hats, all polka-dot,
As whispers weave through pastel night.
While tulips giggle, quite in lots,
In twilight's grip, they shine so bright.

With moonlit charms, the jests set sail,
On breezy winds that carry cheer.
In dim-lit glades, their laughter trails,
As petals sway and tongue-in-cheek appear.

Whispers of the Bloom

The pansies plot in hidden glee,
With mischief tucked behind their layers.
They share their tales with bumblebees,
While daisies spin in flowered prayers.

Cacti stand tall, in prickly pride,
Yet secretly, they wish to dance.
They poke their arms, not very wide,
In desert jokes that dare romance.

With orchids dressed in lavish hats,
They flirt with sunbeams, quite absurd.
In flower beds, a hub of chats,
Each petal knows its punchline word.

So when you stroll past blooms galore,
Remember they're just having fun.
In every color, a joke in store,
As laughter blooms beneath the sun.

The Garden's Lullaby

In a patch of daisies, a squirrel did sing,
He danced with the bees, oh what a silly thing!
Tulips wore hats, and sunflowers wore shoes,
While the carrots played guitar and shared all their blues.

The spinach was laughing, rolling on the ground,
Worms played hide and seek, oh what a funny sound!
The rosebush winked, with petals so bright,
As the garden hummed a tune, deep into the night.

Petal Dreams and Starlit Schemes

The moon wore a crown of blooming white peonies,
While daisies whispered secrets, like busy little bees.
A dandelion puff made wishes take flight,
As the stars twinkled down, sharing giggles of light.

Underneath the night sky, the tulips all sprawled,
With daffodils giggling, oh how they all called!
They plotted a jest, to tickle the moon,
In a garden of dreams, where laughter's in tune.

Secrets Between the Roses

Roses shared whispers, gossiping quite low,
About the irises' dance in the midday glow.
The violets chimed in, with jests oh so bold,
As the lilies laughed lightly, refusing to scold.

A daisy wore glasses, trying to read,
While the peonies giggled at every misdeed.
They plotted a prank on the shy little fern,
In a world made of petals, where laughter would churn.

Where Butterflies Reside

In a land where butterflies flutter and fly,
A caterpillar jokes, though he's quite shy.
His friends, the ladybugs, roll in the grass,
Sharing silly stories, as bright grasses pass.

The flowers were blushing, their colors so bold,
As the blossoms threw parties, and the bees all rolled.
With laughter like sunshine, they danced in the breeze,
In this whimsical world, where joy is a tease.

Jasmine Dreams on Summer Nights

In the garden, a jasmine sings,
With a voice that makes my heart take wings.
Butterflies dance in a clumsy swirl,
They trip on petals, oh what a twirl!

Fireflies blink like tiny stars,
Drunk on nectar from candy bars.
A squirrel debates, should he join the fun?
But he's too busy stealing my bun!

The moon peeks in with a giggling glare,
Spooky shadows popping here and there.
Laughter echoes among the blooms,
As bees throw parties in tiny rooms.

Tonight's the night, let's raise a cheer,
Even the daisies are drinking beer!
Oh, what a sight in this fragrant spree,
Nature's laughter—wild and free!

Mysteries of the Moonlit Garden

Under the moon, secrets unfold,
Tulips gossip, their tales bold.
Roses blush at the juiciest chat,
While daisies wonder, 'What's up with that?'

A toad in a tux says, 'Let's ballroom dance!'
The lilies giggle, forgetting their stance.
Camellias cheer, but one fell asleep,
Dreaming of puddles too big, too deep!

Crickets strum a symphony bright,
As shadows waltz in the pale moonlight.
A bumblebee buzzes with passion so sweet,
But crashes right into the daisies' meet!

Delicate secrets, all wrapped up tight,
In a garden of laughs beneath the starlight.
Oh, who knew flowers could be such a hoot?
In this moonlit garden, they dance in their loot!

Tides of Blooming Whispers

The breeze brings whispers through petals aglow,
A rose tells a tale of a rather big toe!
Lilies lean in, trying not to snicker,
While tulips sweat, competing to flicker.

In this meadow, all merriment thrives,
With daisies debating how to survive.
'Let's sell tickets!' shouts a bold fern,
While a naughty daffodil waits for his turn.

Sunlight giggles, it can't take a pause,
'Who eats the clouds?' asks a curious daws.
Pansies leap up, 'Not us, we are sane!'
And chuckle together in sunshine and rain.

Oh, the tides of mirth roll in and out,
In this garden of joy where flowers shout.
A realm quite silly, with colors so bright,
Come join the dance on a whimsical night!

A Garden of Wishes and Deeds

In a garden of wishes, wild dreams take flight,
Where dandelions scatter with all of their might.
A sunflower winks, 'I wish for a dance!'
While violets giggle, lost in a trance.

The petunias plot to create a bouquet,
But end up in knots, what a silly display.
'Let's raffle a tulip,' whispers a sprout,
As worms roll with laughter, what's that all about?

A clumsy old gnome trips over the grass,
With a hat full of daisies, he hopes none will pass.
The roses all chuckle, while tucking their thorns,
Unruly delights in the garden adorns!

In this playground of plants, come join the mirth,
A joyful brigade, for what it's worth.
Under the sun, with wishes indeed,
In this playful patch, let laughter proceed!

A Garden of Dreams

In a garden where daisies dance,
Bumblebees wear their finest pants.
Tulips giggle as they play,
Waving hello in a sprightly way.

A rose complained, 'I need a hat!'
While orchids pranced, they said, 'How fat!'
The hyacinths whispered secrets bold,
As sunflowers chuckled, 'We're never old!'

Petunias argue over fairies' toast,
While violets boast of their magical boast.
Marigolds paint with laughter and cheer,
In this garden, joy is always near.

With weeds as jesters, making a scene,
Every bloom has a joke, oh so keen.
So come join the fun, don't hesitate,
In a garden where laughter anticipates.

Blossoms in the Breeze

The wind tickles tulips, they giggle with glee,
While daisies gossip, oh, can't you see?
With every flutter, the petals confide,
In this whimsical world, where humor won't hide.

Sunflowers strut like kings on parade,
Lilies laugh as their colors invade.
The breeze plays tricks, it's a playful jest,
Tickling each bloom, it's surely the best!

Roses roll over, they can't take the tease,
While the pansies chuckle, 'We're such a breeze!'
Blooming with mischief, they sway and they sway,
In this garden of giggles, they frolic all day.

So come take a stroll, feel the joy in the air,
With each little blossom, there's laughter to share.
In the sway of the flowers, a funny surprise,
Every petal a joker, under the skies.

The Secret Language of Flowers

In whispers of petals, secrets unfold,
Daisies declare, 'We are bold!'
Roses relay, 'We're the heart's delight,'
While violets giggle, 'We're shy at night!'

Remember the lilies, with mischief to spare,
They joke about lilies that never would dare.
Tulips tease, 'We're the fashion's best friends,'
As daisies chuckle, 'This laughter transcends!'

Cacti complain, 'We're prickly, it's true,'
But within the garden, they banter too.
With laughter unbounded, each petal a muse,
In a world where the flowers just cannot lose.

The pansies conspire, 'Let's start a parade!'
While sunflowers spin in a dizzy charade.
With a wink and a nudge, they send joy unfurled,
In the language of petals, laughter's the world.

Enchanted Petals

In enchanted gardens where petals twist,
Gardening gnomes can't resist.
They juggle daisies, oh what a show,
While roses sing, 'We're the star of the show!'

Marigolds giggle at dandelion tricks,
'Blow us a wish, come on, do quick!'
The hydrangeas wink, 'We're pretty and bright,'
While the daisies shout, 'We're taking flight!'

Every bloom holds a laugh up its sleeve,
With butterflies flitting, taking their leave.
The lilacs tease with scent in the air,
Filling the garden with giggles to share.

As night falls softly, the blooms take a nap,
Whispers of laughter woven in their wrap.
In each charming corner, joy takes its stand,
In this whimsical world, laughter's so grand!

Echoing Footsteps in the Garden

In the garden, shoes go clomp,
The daisies giggle, then they stomp.
A butterfly with shades on bright,
Is throwing quite the silly sight.

Worms wear hats, and off they march,
Planting seeds while holding arch.
The sunflowers wink, oh what a show,
As daisies plot a dance below.

Bees buzz loudly, with tiny beats,
Humming along to silly tweets.
Ferris wheel blooms spin around,
Joyful chaos is what they've found.

In each petal, laughter shines,
Each step a story, life aligns.
With every echo, giggles bloom,
In this garden, there's always room.

The Dance of the Daisies

Daisies gathered, ready to sway,
Through their petals, they will play.
With a twist and a little jig,
They laugh and shout, oh what a gig!

A ladybug joins the wild spree,
In a tutu, oh so carefree.
The sun shines bright, a spotlight grand,
As daisies twirl in a funny band.

They trip and slip on dewy leaves,
A bouquet of smiles, nothing deceives.
With a hiccup here and a snort there,
The daisies dance without a care.

Round and round, 'neath the blue sky,
Hilarity blooms, oh my, oh my!
With every leap, they shout with glee,
In this garden, they're wild and free.

Flora's Dreamweaver

In dreams, flowers wear silly hats,
While chatting gaily with the cats.
They share jokes, oh what a scene,
Petals laughing, bright and green.

Tulips twist, doing the tango,
They stomp their roots, and off they go!
Sunsets decked in dazzling hues,
Steal their spotlight, sipping brews.

A rogue breeze plays peek-a-boo,
Tossing petals, like confetti too.
In this dream, nothing's amiss,
With every bloom, there's a blissful kiss.

As sleepy bees begin to snooze,
The moon whispers dreams to the hues.
With nightly giggles, they softly weave,
A tangle of laughter, we believe.

Beneath the Canopy of Color

Under rainbow canopies, we sit,
With flowers gossiping, won't admit.
The roses boast of their grand size,
While violets snicker, oh what lies!

Beneath the petals, secrets flow,
As bumblebees waltz, stealing the show.
In this riot of hues and scents,
Nature's humor is what condense.

Twiggy trees with faces sprout,
Cheering on plants when they pout.
Their leaves ruffle with every breeze,
In laughter, we find the sweetest tease.

In this garden, giggles reign supreme,
Each bloom a part of the comic dream.
So join the fun beneath the sun,
Where colors blend, and we all run!

The Timeless Call of Petals

In a garden full of chatter,
The daisies wore a silly hat.
Sunflowers danced to a tune,
While lilacs played with the cat.

Rosy cheeks on tulips bright,
Swirling like they're in a game.
Butterflies in a dizzy fight,
Chasing after a wandering flame.

Pansies giggle, the violets mock,
With each bloom, a giggle spills.
Bees buzzing with a ticking clock,
Pollinating all the thrills.

With petals soft, they plot and scheme,
To tickle noses, cause a sneeze.
Each budding bloom, a funny dream,
Nature's jesters, they aim to please.

Enchanted Realm of Green Dreams

In the land of leaves so green,
Where ivy plays hide-and-seek.
Witty weeds plot a grand scene,
   As ferns giggle with a peek.

Mossy carpets, soft and fluffy,
Where daisies jest and make a fuss.
Laughter spills, it's never stuffy,
   Watch out for that bouncy bus!

Cacti join in, their prickles shine,
Telling jokes that might just sting.
Tulips giggle, oh how divine,
   In a jestful, joyful spring.

The trees sway wearing leafy crowns,
   Their swaying arms do tickle too.
A playful dance in nature's gowns,
   A silly world where laughter grew.

The Spirit of Blossoming Fields

In fields where flowers leap and play,
The poppies're cracking silly jokes.
Dandelions dance in sunny sway,
While clovers tease and poke at folks.

Honeysuckle giggles all around,
As corny puns take flower form.
Every fragrance is a sound,
In this garden, joy is the norm.

Morning glories climb up tall,
Reaching high for a cloud or two.
Their vibrant voices rise and call,
To tickle morning's golden dew.

With petals bright, they bumble near,
The spirit of fun is ever near.
In blooming fields, we laugh and cheer,
For nature's jesters, let's all hear!

Lullabies of the Colorful Dawn

With dawn's first light, the flowers yawn,
In hues that tickle the waking sun.
Peonies stretch, their petals drawn,
While marigolds prepare for fun.

Pansies burst with laughter's grace,
Composing tunes, a funny choir.
Zinnias dance, a bubbly race,
In sunny skies, we all conspire.

Morning glories, bright and bold,
Tell tales of dreams in soft, sweet tones.
A jester's heart in colors rolled,
As joy is sown in garden zones.

In this dawn of petals bright,
The world awakens, chuckles fly.
Nature's tunes, a pure delight,
In sleepy blooms, we laugh, not sigh.

Gardens of the Imagination

In a garden filled with candy,
Plastic flowers all quite dandy.
The daisies wink with gummy smiles,
While lollipops stand in tight lines.

Bees wear hats and glasses too,
Chasing butterflies that stick like glue.
Caterpillars bounce on trampolines,
As frogs croak out their rap routines.

A snail races on a skateboard fast,
While chocolate vines are growing vast.
In this land where laughter's the key,
A petunia sings in perfect glee.

So come and play in colors bright,
Where every petal beams with light.
In this place of magic dreams,
The world is brighter than it seems.

The Realm of Blooming Whimsy

In a land where sunflowers dance,
They wear polka dots by chance.
The tulips giggle, wave their heads,
While roses joke about their beds.

The daisies throw a picnic prank,
Hiding ants beneath a tank.
Bold violets flip in sheer delight,
As pansies plan to fly a kite.

Beetles wearing tiny shoes,
Strut their stuff, no other views.
A hedgehog dons a bowler hat,
Sipping tea while saying, "What's that?"

Join the fun where laughter flows,
Through garden paths where anything goes.
With petals bright and jokes to share,
The whimsies bloom beyond compare.

Hues of Serenity

Blushing petals in colors bright,
Whisper secrets in soft moonlight.
Lavender chuckles, spreading cheer,
While bluebells chime, "Come gather near!"

In fields where every color sings,
A butterfly flaps, doing bling-bling.
Marigolds strut in yellow gowns,
While delphiniums wear frowning crowns.

The sunflowers paint the cloudy skies,
With splashes of laughter and silly sighs.
Lilies launch a playful fight,
With petals flying in pure delight.

Amid this tapestry of hues,
Nature giggles, sharing few clues.
A canvas crafted with whimsies bright,
Where colors swirl, a pure delight.

Nature's Embrace

In nature's arms, the flowers grin,
With tulip hats and bold chagrin.
The daisies dance in silly rhymes,
Tickling bees with their silly chimes.

As daffodils play hopscotch near,
They shout, "We're winning!" with loud cheer.
Petunias prance in marching bands,
While poppies juggle with their hands.

Hummingbirds serve tea in flight,
While roses debate what's wrong or right.
In this garden where mischief reigns,
Laughter travels through the lanes.

So join the fun, don't hesitate,
In this land where joy won't wait.
Nature's arms are wide and free,
With humor wrapped in harmony.

Radiance in Lavender Hues

In a garden of lavender, bees twirl and sway,
They dance on the flowers, oh what a display!
With pollen on noses, they giggle and tease,
Who knew bees could dance with such finesse and ease?

Purple rain showers when the clouds start to cry,
Flowers wear raindrops like jewels in the sky.
In lavender pools, the bunnies all float,
Plotting their mischief aboard a sweet boat.

Lavender shampoo makes everyone smell,
But squirrels just laugh and they run off to tell.
They whisper and murmur, "What's that dopey scent?"
As they plot a new prank, in a flower they're bent.

With petals as pillows, they take to the air,
Bouncing and flipping without a care.
A riot of color, a giggling spree,
In this world of absurdity, come join us, whee!

The Petal Alchemist's Tale

Once there was a flower with magical bloom,
A wizard thought, "Great! I'll make it perfume!"
He mixed up the petals with a wink and a grin,
But ended up sneezing, and chaos begin.

Petals turned purple, then bright shiny gold,
Everyone in the garden grew bolder and bold.
The daisies started prancing, the roses sang loud,
While the shy little lilies hid under a cloud.

He conjured up laughter with a sprinkle of cheer,
Now flowers throw parties at night, oh dear!
With gnomes as the DJ, and fairies on lights,
The garden turns wild on those starry nights.

But be cautious of blooms that chuckle and tease,
They might give you hiccups or tickle your knees.
A potion of giggles will burst from the core,
And keep you forever coming back for more!

Veils of Sweet Scent

In the land of aromas, where flowers collide,
A bouquet of whispers begins to confide.
The lilacs exchange secrets with the old sunflowers,
Holding court under trees for hours and hours.

A daffodil snickers, "I smell like delight!"
While geraniums gossip and dance through the night.
With scents in the air that twirl like a dancer,
They plot to make perfumes that smell like a prancer.

The roses, quite nosey, are always in tow,
Chasing down scents, but they're slipping in snow.
"Watch out for those daisies!" the pansies all squeal,
"For they'll make you giggle and twirl like a wheel!"

As pollen floats by, making everyone sneeze,
The garden erupts in a chorus of wheezes.
But amidst all the chaos, a sweet fragrance lingers,
Bringing smiles like sunshine upon every finger.

Garden of Ethereal Whimsy

In a garden so strange, where the odd flowers play,
The tulips wear glasses to see through the spray.
The zinnias chuckle, sporting hats oh so big,
While the snapdragons snap at each whimsical jig.

Butterflies argue about polka-dot flair,
While the mushrooms gossip, all stylishly bare.
A petunia in sneakers races quick as a fox,
"Catch me if you can!" she giggles, "Silly rocks!"

The sunflowers debate who's the tallest of all,
As spindly sweet stalks hold their heads proud and tall.
A dandelion sings with the grass acting sly,
To challenge the breeze to a dance in the sky.

With laughter and color in whimsical sights,
The garden holds parties that last through the nights.
So come join the fray, let your spirit be light,
In this fanciful garden, everything feels right!

Echoes of Colorful Dreams

In a garden where daisies play,
Tulips dance in a bright ballet.
Sunflowers wink with golden glee,
Singing secrets to the honeybee.

Petunias giggle, teasing the breeze,
While violets spin tales with ease.
Marigolds prance in a colorful row,
As the roses blush, putting on a show.

Larkspur whispers to the busy bees,
"Come join the fun, share your sweet tease!"
The irises wink, with playful charms,
Creating laughter in flowered arms.

Dandelions float like tiny dreams,
Tickling the toes of racing streams.
In this wild patch of joys untold,
Every bloom is a story bold.

Selves Entwined in Vines

In a tangle of twirls and loops,
Vines celebrate with tiny whoops.
Grapevines giggle, wearing green hats,
While climbing roses chat with the bats.

A wisteria swings, all purple and grand,
Tickling each leaf with a delicate hand.
Morning glories boast, 'We're the best crew!'
As they stretch and yawn, getting their due.

The ivy whispers sweet, leafy dreams,
Daring the blooms to join in teams.
Sunlight has fun, casting playful rays,
While the tangled trellis sways and sways.

In this garden, a raucous scene,
Vines and flowers share ice cream.
Chasing their shadows, they leap and dive,
In a jolly world, where all are alive.

A Tapestry of Fragrance

Scented whispers fill the air,
With minty giggles everywhere.
Lavender dances, a calming trend,
While rosemary schemes with a wink to send.

Cinnamon barks, in a spicy chat,
Jasmine's laughter is where it's at.
Beside the daisies, sweet scents collide,
Tickling noses with joy as they glide.

Peonies skip with their rosy pride,
As chamomile sways, not one to hide.
Fennel's humor, sharp and bright,
Makes the garden a hilarious sight.

In fragrant halls, where aromas play,
Even the soil joins the ballet.
This tapestry spins tales of delight,
Where scents burst forth, morning till night.

Secrets of the Sunlit Meadow

In meadows bright, where secrets blend,
Butterflies flutter, the skies they bend.
A patchwork quilt of blooms so bold,
Giggling friends in a dance they hold.

The grass tickles knees in the sun,
As daisies laugh when the day's begun.
Frolicsome friends, the bees buzz along,
In this meadow, everyone's strong.

The lilies gossip, sharing their tales,
As dragonflies zip with shimmering trails.
Tall grasses sway, a comical show,
Inviting all creatures to join and flow.

In the light where giggles roam free,
Nature creates its own jubilee.
With laughter and joy, this meadow sways,
A secret realm where humor stays.

www.ingramcontent.com/pod-product-compliance
Lightning Source LLC
Chambersburg PA
CBHW071815160426
43209CB00003B/95